Electricity

Nicolas Brasch

Rigby®

www.Rigby.com
1-800-531-5015

Rigby Focus Forward

This Edition © 2009 Rigby, a Harcourt Education Imprint

Published in 2007 by Nelson Australia Pty Ltd ACN: 058 280 149
A Cengage Learning company

1 2 3 4 5 6 7 8 374 14 13 12 11 10 09 08 07
Printed and bound in China

Electricity
ISBN-13   978-1-4190-3823-5
ISBN-10   1-4190-3823-0

Acknowledgments
Illustrations by Boris Silvestri
The author and publisher would like to acknowledge permission to reproduce material from the following sources:
Photographs by Corbis/DK Limited, p. 21; iStockphoto, pp. 4 top, 23 bottom/ Jiblet, p. 10 right/ Anna Sirotina, p. 17/ Moritz Van Hacht, cover, p. 12; Photolibrary, p. 20/ 4x5 Coll-Francisoc Cruz, p. 22/ AJ Photo/SPL, pp. 3, 23 top right/ Chagnon, p. 9/ David R Frazier, p. 4 bottom/ Freid/Whisenhunt, p. 23 left/ Jeremy Walker/SPL, back cover, p. 19/ Malcolm Fife, p. 16/ Mark Burnett, p. 13/ Photo Inc, p. 10 left/ Sheila Terry, p. 14/ Simon Fraser, p. 18/ SPL, pp. 5, 11 inset/ The Bridgeman Art Library, pp. 11, 12 inset/Xxxxxxx Xxxxxxx/ Van D Bucher, p. 15/ Science Photo Library, p. 7/ Adam Hart-Davis, p. 20 inset/ David Nicholls, pp. 8 left, 8 right.

Electricity

Nicolas Brasch

Contents

Chapter 1

INTRODUCING ELECTRICITY

Electricity is a form of energy.
It is all around us.
Today most people around the world
use electricity every day
to power lots of different things.
People use electricity at home, school, work,
and in the car.

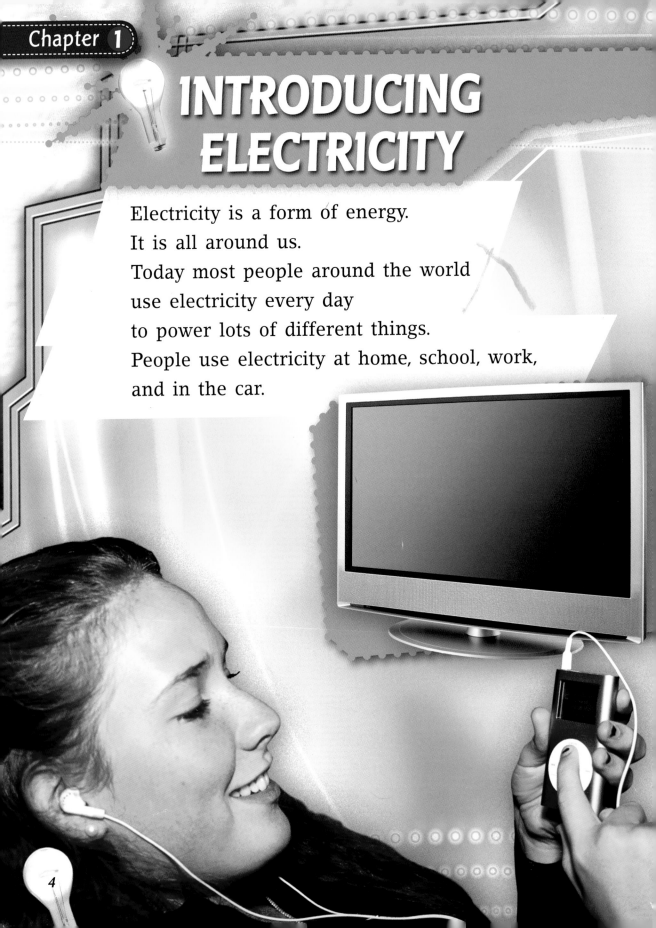

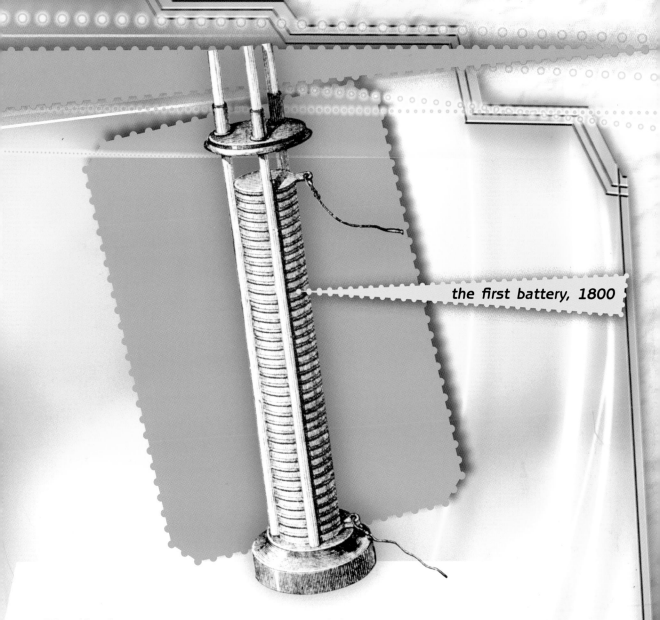

Until about 200 years ago, nothing was powered
by electricity.
In the past, people knew about electricity,
but they didn't know how to use its power.
Static electricity was the first form of electricity
to be discovered.
It wasn't until the invention of the **battery**, in 1800,
that current electricity was discovered.

Chapter 2

WHAT IS ELECTRICITY?

Scientists have found that electricity is the movement of electrons between atoms.

Otto von Guericke working his electrostatic generator, 1663.

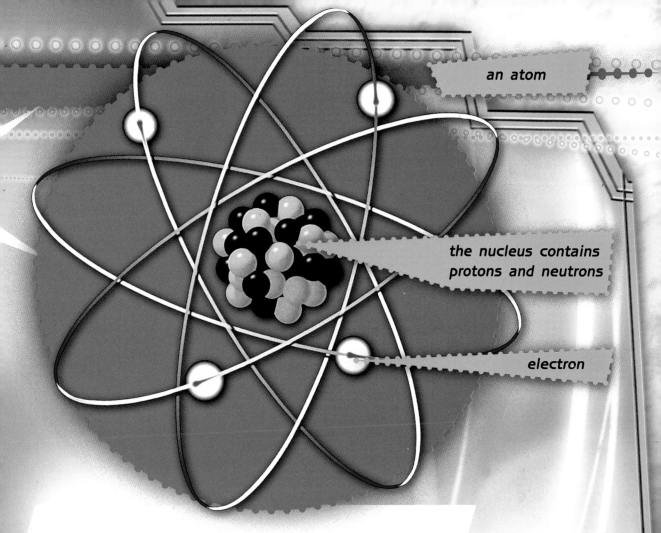

an atom

the nucleus contains protons and neutrons

electron

Everything on Earth is made of atoms,
which are very small particles.
In the early 1900s, scientists found that atoms
are made of even smaller particles.
They discovered that atoms have a tiny core, or center,
which is called a nucleus.
Inside the nucleus are protons, which
have a positive electrical charge,
and neutrons, which have no electrical charge.
Spinning around the nucleus are more tiny particles
called electrons, which have a negative electrical charge.

While doing experiments with atoms, scientists wondered what kept the electrons spinning around the nucleus.

They discovered that the force of attraction between the positively charged protons and negatively charged electrons keeps the electrons spinning.

This made sense to the scientists because they had observed that positively charged things and negatively charged things are attracted to each other.

electron

an atom

an atom

Electrons move between atoms and therefore create electricity.

But what really interested scientists about electrons is that they can move among atoms and, as a result, create electricity.

Today scientists and engineers use this knowledge
to come up with ways to get electrons
to move between atoms to make
amazing, new inventions that can make our lives easier.

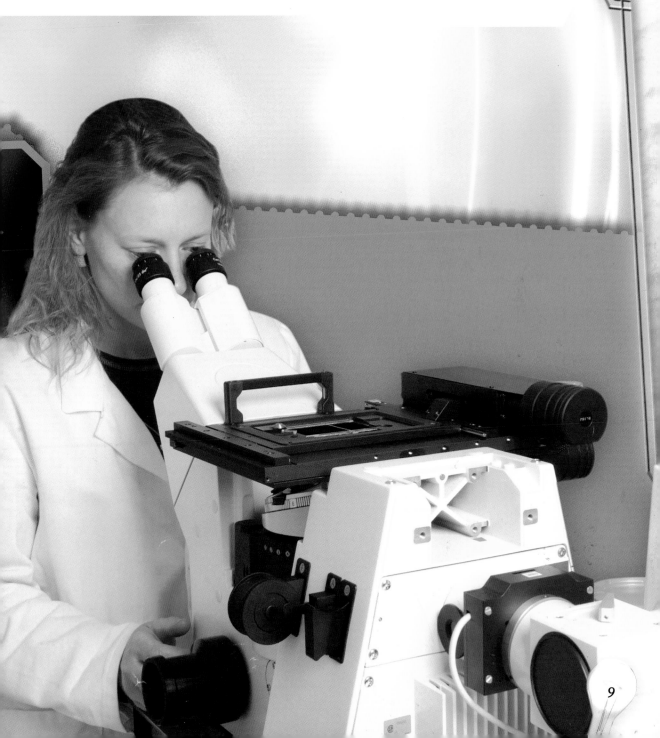

Chapter 3

DISCOVERING STATIC ELECTRICITY

Thales of Miletus was one of the first people
to write about the experiments that he did with electricity.
Thales lived more than 2,500 years ago in ancient Greece.
Some historians say that he rubbed a piece of **amber**
on a piece of sheepskin.
Then he held the amber close to pieces of dried grass.
The grass jumped up and stuck to the amber.
The same thing happened when he held the amber
close to feathers.

amber

Thales of Miletus

Dr. William Gilbert

In 1600 Dr. William Gilbert, an Englishman, found that when he rubbed glass, wax, and rubber, things would stick to them, too.
What Thales of Miletus and Dr. Gilbert had found was static electricity.

What Is Static Electricity?

Static electricity is a form of electricity that is caused by **friction**.

Friction occurs when two objects are rubbed together. Thales of Miletus caused friction when he rubbed amber with sheepskin.

This friction caused the balance of positive and negative charges to change and resulted in an electrical charge.

Thales of Miletus

Lightning is a form of static electricity.

While static electricity doesn't run in a steady current,
it can leap from one object to another.
When people come in contact with static electricity,
it can make their hair stand on end!

Chapter 4

DISCOVERING CURRENT ELECTRICITY

Over the next few centuries, other scientists kept experimenting with electricity. One of them was an Italian scientist named Alessandro Volta.

Alessandro Volta

In 1800 Alessandro Volta did experiments with
metal disks and fabric soaked in acid.
When he connected the metal disks with a piece of wire,
an electric current occurred.
Volta's stack of disks, metals, and fabrics
was the first battery.

Electric Currents

An electric current occurs when the movement between atoms happens at the same time and in the same direction.
An electric current is a flow of electrons in a wire.

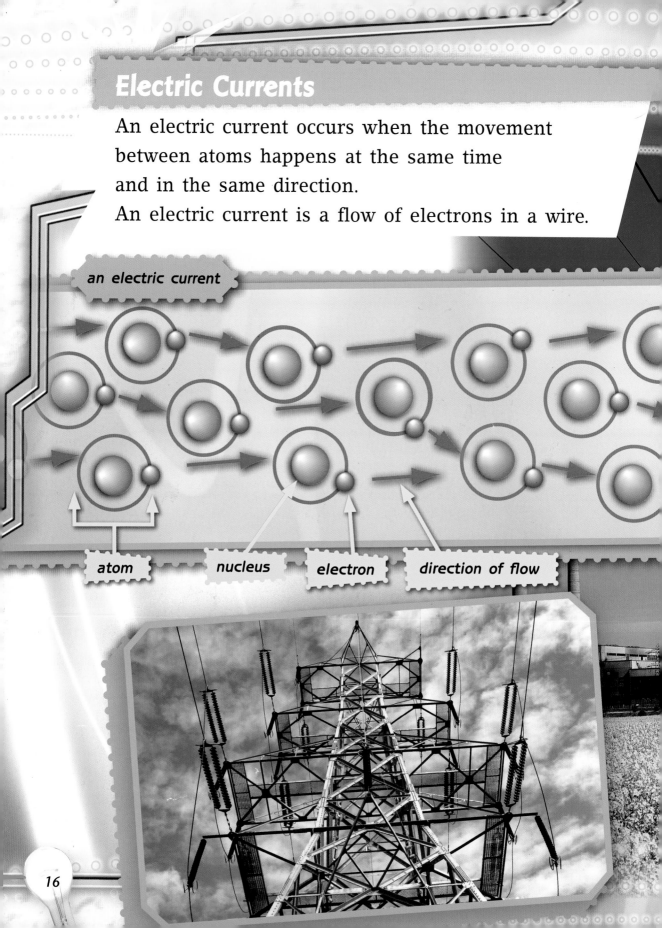

an electric current

atom

nucleus

electron

direction of flow

Today wires are used to transmit electric currents from power plants to our homes, businesses, and schools.

direction of electric current

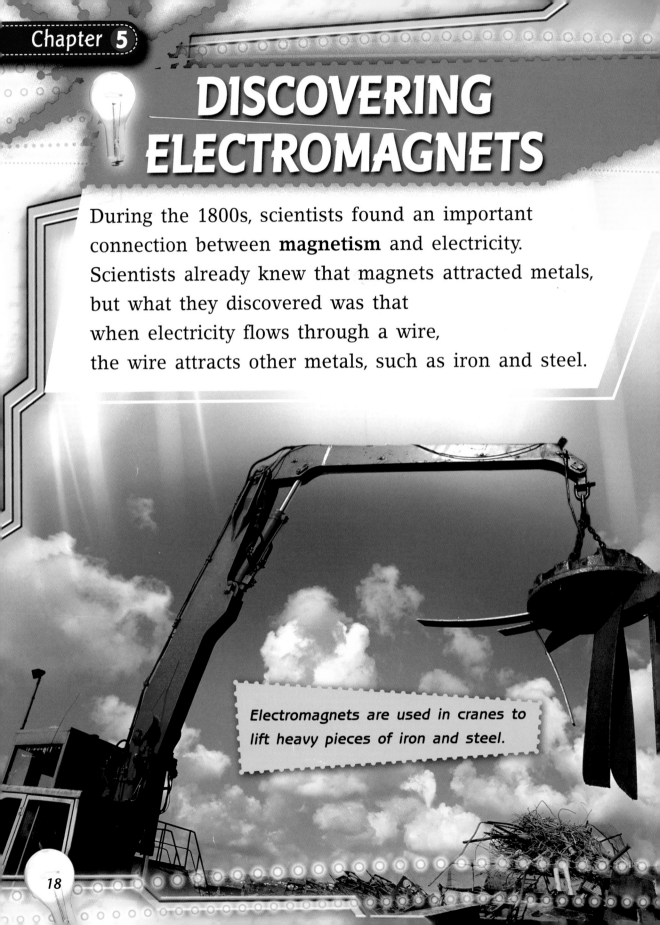

Chapter 5

DISCOVERING ELECTROMAGNETS

During the 1800s, scientists found an important connection between **magnetism** and electricity. Scientists already knew that magnets attracted metals, but what they discovered was that when electricity flows through a wire, the wire attracts other metals, such as iron and steel.

Electromagnets are used in cranes to lift heavy pieces of iron and steel.

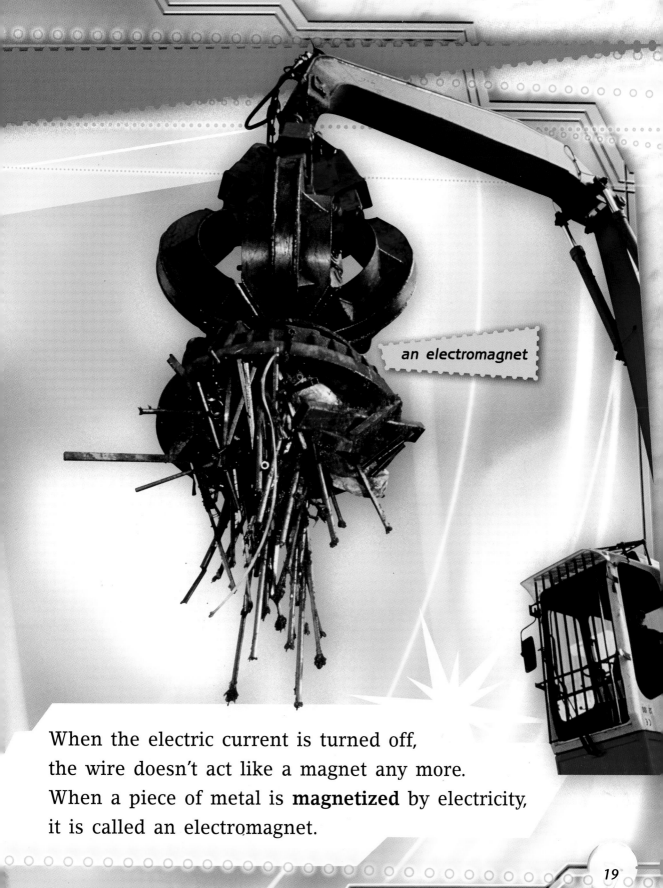

an electromagnet

When the electric current is turned off,
the wire doesn't act like a magnet any more.
When a piece of metal is **magnetized** by electricity,
it is called an electromagnet.

Chapter 6

MICHAEL FARADAY

One scientist who made an important contribution to electricity was Michael Faraday, an Englishman. In 1831 Faraday knew that electricity could make wire and metal act like a magnet.
What was unknown to him was whether a magnet could be used to make electricity.

a wire coil used by Faraday

Michael Faraday

Faraday conducted many experiments.
He found that if he moved a strong magnet
past a coil of wire,
electrons would flow through the wire.

Faraday's wire
coil experiment

Faraday also built the first electric generator—
a machine that uses a magnet to produce electricity.
Faraday's discovery allows today's power stations
to make electricity.

Chapter 7

ELECTRICITY TODAY

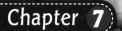

Life for people throughout most of the world
is unimaginable without electricity.
There are so many things that we couldn't do
if we didn't have electricity—
watch television, play computer games, listen to music,
drive cars, do work, and heat and cool homes
and workplaces.

Today the demand for electrical power is greater than ever before, and it continues to grow. Scientists and engineers will continue the development of new ways to make and use electricity.

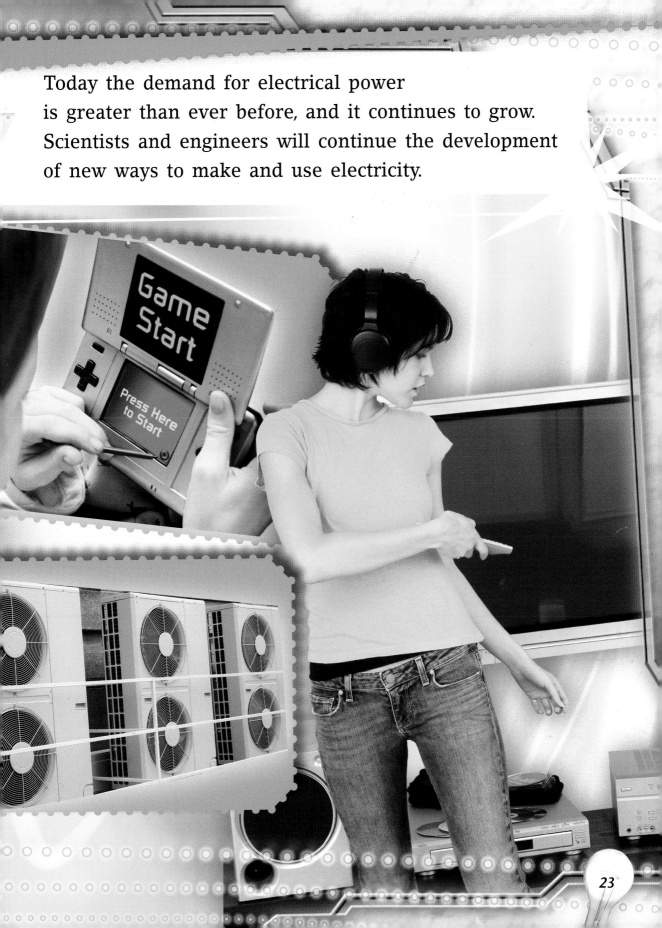

Glossary

amber   a hard, clear fossilized resin. Amber is usually a honey color

battery   a device that stores energy and turns it into electricity

friction   the resistance an object encounters when rubbed over another object

magnetized   something possessing magnetic qualities

magnetism   the ability to attract or repel

Index